Rookie
Read-About®
Civics

We Are
Good Citizens

Ann Bonwill

Content Consultant
Elizabeth Case DeSantis, M.A. Elementary Education
Julia A. Stark Elementary School, Stamford, Connecticut

Reading Consultant
Jeanne M. Clidas, Ph.D.
Reading Specialist

Children's Press®
An Imprint of Scholastic Inc.

Library of Congress Cataloging-in-Publication Data

Names: Bonwill, Ann, author.
Title: We are good citizens / by Ann Bonwill.
Description: New York, NY : Children's Press, An Imprint of Scholastic Inc.,
    2019. | Series: Rookie read-about civics | Includes index.
Identifiers: LCCN 2018027246| ISBN 9780531129135 (library binding) | ISBN
    9780531137710 (pbk.)
Subjects: LCSH: Citizenship–Juvenile literature.
Classification: LCC JF801 .B575 2019 | DDC 323.6–dc23

Produced by Spooky Cheetah Press
Design: Keith Plechaty/kwpCreative
Creative Direction: Judith E. Christ for Scholastic Inc.

Published in 2019 by Children's Press, an imprint of Scholastic Inc.

Printed in North Mankato, MN, USA   113

1 2 3 4 5 6 7 8 9 10 R 28   27 26 25 24 23 22 21 20 19

Scholastic, Inc., 557 Broadway, New York, NY 10012.

Photos © cover: FatCamera/Getty Images; cover flag bunting: LiveStock/Shutterstock; 3: Ariel Skelley/Getty Images; 4 top: Elyse Lewin/Getty Images; 4 bottom left: FatCamera/iStockphoto; 4 bottom right: filadendron/iStockphoto; 7: Ariel Skelley/Getty Images; 9: BONEKphoto/Alamy Images; 10: Hero Images/Getty Images; 13: Stephanie Rausser/ Getty Images; 15: MNStudio/iStockphoto; 16: Creatas/Getty Images; 19: Image Source/age fotostock; 21: Hutchings/ PhotoEdit; 22: Kevin Dodge/Getty Images; 25: Rawpixel.com/Shutterstock; 27: Christian Oth/Getty Images; 28-29: Lyudmyla Kharlamova/Shutterstock; 29 top: Ilike/Shutterstock; 29 bottom right: Aaron Amat/Shutterstock; 30 top left: Sawitree Pamee/Getty Images; 30 center: RichLegg/Getty Images; 30 bottom left: Andersen Ross/Getty Images; 30 bottom right: bst2012/iStockphoto; 31 top right: Elyse Lewin/Getty Images; 31 center right group of kids: Ariel Skelley/ Getty Images; 31 center right mopping: Richard Hutchings/PhotoEdit; 31 bottom right: Rawpixel.com/Shutterstock; 32: DebbiSmirnoff/iStockphoto.

Table of Contents

CHAPTER 1

We Belong!

What is a citizen? A citizen is a person who belongs in a group.

We are all citizens.

We are citizens of our families, our schools, and our **communities**. We are citizens of the world.

What groups do you belong in?

As citizens, we have rights.

A right is something that everyone deserves to have.

We have the right to live in a safe and healthy neighborhood. We have the right to read books in a quiet library and play together in a clean park.

 Do kids have rights?

As citizens, we also have responsibilities.

Responsibilities are things that we are supposed to do.

We have the responsibility to return our books to the library so other people can enjoy them. We pick up after our pets so the park stays clean.

 What are some of your responsibilities?

CHAPTER 2

In Our Family

We are citizens of our family.

We have the right to live together in a clean and tidy home. Would you like to sit on a couch full of crumbs or eat dinner next to a pile of dirty socks?

We have the responsibility to do our part by cleaning up after ourselves.

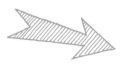 Why is it important to keep the kitchen clean?

Sometimes we are happy. Sometimes we are sad. We have the right to share these feelings with our families. We have the right to be heard.

When we share, we use kind words and speak nicely. We listen respectfully when others share their feelings with us.

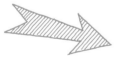 How can you show that you are listening?

We have the right to be treated kindly by our families.

We treat others kindly, too. We carry groceries for our parents and take turns on the swing with our cousins. We show kindness by sharing toys, giving hugs, and offering help.

 How can you help a relative like a younger sibling or a grandparent?

CHAPTER 3

At School

We are citizens of our school. We have the right to learn at school.

In order to learn as much as we can, we pay attention in class. We listen to the teacher and ask questions. It is our responsibility to do our homework.

We have the right to be safe at school. Teachers and other grown-ups help to keep us safe.

But we have to help, too. In order to be safe, we follow the rules and listen to directions. We push in our chairs and walk, not run, in the halls.

 What would happen if there were no rules at school?

We have the right to be included at school. It does not feel good to be left out.

We include others when playing and learning. It is important to work together and **cooperate**.

What can you do if a classmate is cleaning up after art class?

CHAPTER 4

In the World

We are citizens of the world.

We are lucky to live in a world full of **diversity**. People speak different languages, eat different foods, and wear different clothing.

We respect differences and are friendly to everyone we meet.

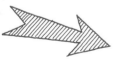 Does anyone in your class speak more than one language?

We have the right to live in a clean and healthy world. Our world needs help to stay clean.

We respect the **environment** by taking care of nature.

 What can you do to take care of Earth?

We belong in many different groups. It feels good to belong. We have rights, but we also have responsibilities. To be part of a community, we need to fulfill our responsibilities.

We are good citizens!

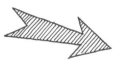 How are community helpers good citizens?

Learning to Compromise

As citizens, we are kind and work together.
But what happens when we don't agree?
We can solve problems peacefully
when we are honest and take turns.
That is what it means to compromise.

1. You want to play basketball, but your friend wants to play tag.

What should you do?

2. You and your friend are working together on a science project. She wants to write about volcanoes and you want to write about earthquakes.

What should you do?

3. You accidentally ripped your friend's paper. He thinks someone else ripped it.

What should you do?

If you are having trouble solving a problem, put yourself in the other person's shoes. When you imagine what someone else is feeling, it can help you see things in a new way.

Be a Good Citizen!

How can you help on the way to school?

◀**Picking up litter on the sidewalk**

▼**Holding the door for someone**

◀**Helping someone cross the street**

▶**Handing the newspaper to your neighbor**

communities (kuh-**myoo**-ni-teez):
places and the people who live in them
▶ *We are citizens of our families, our schools, and our* **communities***.*

cooperate (koh-**ah**-puh-rate):
to work together toward the same goal
▶ *It is important to work together and* **cooperate***.*

diversity (di-**vur**-si-tee):
a variety
▶ *In a world full of* **diversity***, people eat different foods and wear different clothing.*

environment (en-**vye**-ruhn-muhnt):
the natural surroundings of living things, such as the air, land, or sea
▶ *We respect the* **environment** *by taking care of nature.*

Index

Facts for Now

Visit this Scholastic website to learn more about the We Are Good Citizens:

www.factsfornow.scholastic.com

Enter the keywords **Citizens**

About the Author

Ann Bonwill enjoys writing books for children. She is a citizen of Virginia, where she lives with her husband, her son, and a corgi named Arthur.